STRAIGHT TALK

P9-CEL-560
FOR KIDS

The Truth About Food

Stephanie Paris

Consultants

Timothy Rasinski, Ph.D.
Kent State University

Lori Oczkus
Literacy Consultant

Dana Lambrose, M.S.N., PMHNP
West Coast University

Based on writing from
TIME For Kids. *TIME For Kids* and the *TIME For Kids* logo are registered trademarks of TIME Inc. Used under license.

Publishing Credits

Dona Herweck Rice, *Editor-in-Chief*
Lee Aucoin, *Creative Director*
Jamey Acosta, *Senior Editor*
Lexa Hoang, *Designer*
Stephanie Reid, *Photo Editor*
Rachelle Cracchiolo, *M.S.Ed., Publisher*

Image Credits: p.35 Timothy J. Bradley/
Stephanie Reid; p.17 Kelly Brownlee/
Stephanie Reid; p.15 Choosemyplate.gov;
p.11 (bottom) Anne Regan Greenleaf
via. Flickr; p.14 (right) MyPyramid.gov;
p.14 (left) National Nutrition Guide;
p.38 Newscom; All other images from
Shutterstock.

Teacher Created Materials

5301 Oceanus Drive
Huntington Beach, CA 92649-1030
http://www.tcmpub.com
ISBN 978-1-4333-4857-0
© 2013 Teacher Created Materials, Inc.
Printed in China
YiCai.032019.CA201901471

Table of Contents

Fuel for Life

What do you like to do? Do you like to play soccer, or do you prefer to read adventure stories? Maybe you like video games, dancing, or just talking with your friends. No matter what you enjoy, your body needs energy and the right building blocks to make it. Our bodies get what they need through eating. But your body can't form the building blocks to make a healthy body if you don't eat healthy foods.

What happens when you don't eat right? Eating too much of the wrong food can be harmful. Eating too much of any food can lead to weight issues. And eating too little of the right foods can lead to poor **nutrition**. So how can we choose the right foods?

THINK LINK

1 What kinds of foods are healthiest for your body?

2 How do you give your body energy?

3 How can you make healthier choices in your life?

Every Body, Every Day

We get the nutrients we need to **thrive** in many ways. Everyone needs to drink water. Everyone needs to eat a variety of foods to stay healthy. It's also important to remember that every body is a little different. Babies need different foods than older kids. Someone who is bigger and very active will need more food than someone who is small and sits a lot. **Allergies**, body type, and personal taste all affect what we need to eat.

COUNTING CALORIES

A **calorie** is a unit of energy. Some foods have a lot of calories. Others have very few. You can find out how many calories are in a serving by reading food packaging or looking online. Most kids need between 1,600–2,500 calories each day.

BODY BASICS

WHAT WE NEED	WHY WE NEED IT
Protein	Human bodies need **protein** to replace cells that have worn out and died. And you need protein to help you grow!
Vitamins and Minerals	Your body gets weak and sick if you don't get enough **vitamins** and **minerals**. But be careful! There are some that can make you sick if you have too much.
Fatty Acids	These are a special type of fat your body needs but cannot make on its own.
Calories	This is energy. Your body needs enough calories to do all the things you do in a day. But you don't want to eat too much, or your body may store fat.
Fiber	**Fiber** keeps your **digestive tract** clean and makes sure foods move through the system smoothly.

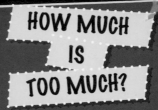

DIG DEEPER!

HOW MUCH IS TOO MUCH?

Eating the right foods is only one part of the puzzle. It's also important to eat the right amounts. Many restaurants like to make customers feel as if they are getting a good deal by putting a LOT of food on the plate. But that isn't healthy. Some restaurant meals serve more than an entire day's worth of calories on one plate! Check out these healthy portion sizes.

A bagel should be about the size of a can of tuna.

Dried fruit is high in calories. A serving is the size of a golf ball.

A cup of rice is about the same size as a light bulb.

A single serving of meat is the same size as a deck of cards.

Rise and Shine

Breakfast is the most important meal of the day. *Fast* means "to not eat." So to *break fast* means "to eat again after not eating during the night."

Overnight, your body works hard while you sleep. It builds new cells and fixes things that were damaged. To start your day, you need fuel, but not just any fuel. It's especially important that you eat healthy foods for breakfast. Your body has used up a lot of energy and nutrients from the food you ate yesterday. If you don't eat a good breakfast, you will probably feel tired all day.

SMART START

Want to get an *A* on that test? Eat your breakfast! Many studies have shown that kids who eat a good breakfast every day do better in school. And kids who eat a good breakfast before a test get better scores!

BREAKFAST AROUND the WORLD

There's more than one way to eat a great breakfast. Around the world, people love to wake up to delicious food. Breakfasts with protein help everyone power through until lunch.

In Mexico, many people enjoy eggs and tortillas in the morning.

In South Korea, people eat a hearty soup for breakfast.

Russians often eat black rye bread, eggs, pickles, and cured meats.

In Cameroon, people eat beignets (BEN-yayz), a kind of doughnut, with beans.

SUGAR BLUES

When you eat something sweet for breakfast, it gives your body a quick burst of energy. But that energy gets used up fast. When your sugar levels shoot up and come down quickly, your body gets stressed. You can wind up feeling tired and cranky. Eating whole grains, proteins, and less sugar can help.

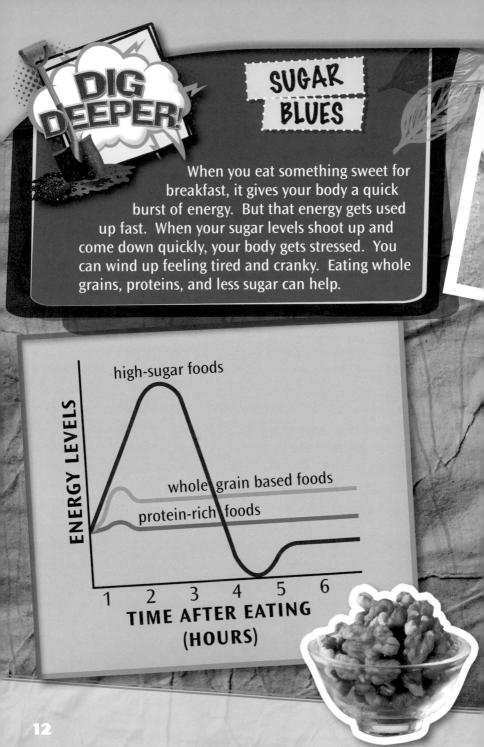

ENERGY LEVELS

high-sugar foods

whole grain based foods

protein-rich foods

1 2 3 4 5 6

TIME AFTER EATING (HOURS)

LINE UP!

Ingredients are required to be listed on packages in order from most to least used. Watch out for some of the different names sugar goes by: *brown sugar, agave nectar, corn syrup, molasses, honey,* or *malt syrup.*

BEFORE BED

If your blood sugar shoots up and then crashes late in the night, you may have trouble sleeping. Trade in sweet snacks and drinks for those that will help you sleep. Substitute soda, apple juice, or cookies with lean proteins such as nuts or milk.

MyPlate

The United States Department of Agriculture (USDA) has a guide to help people eat a healthy diet. MyPlate is one tool you can use to make decisions about what you eat. It shows how much of each kind of food you should eat each day. Following MyPlate can help you get the nutrients and energy your body needs.

If you look at the plate on page 15, you will see that half of it is filled with fruits and **vegetables**. So when you fill your plate at mealtime, try to cover half of it with fruits and vegetables. Try to make sure the grains you eat are rich in nutrients. And look for dairy and proteins such as fish that are low in fat.

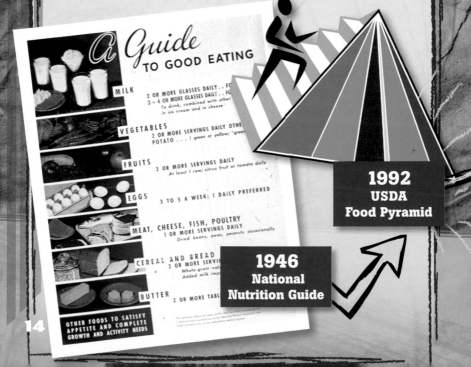

A Guide TO GOOD EATING

MILK 2 OR MORE GLASSES DAILY.. FO
3 - 4 OR MORE GLASSES DAILY .. FO
To drink, combined with other
in ice cream and in cheese

VEGETABLES 2 OR MORE SERVINGS DAILY OTHE
POTATO . . . 1 green or yellow; "gree

FRUITS 2 OR MORE SERVINGS DAILY
At least 1 raw; citrus fruit or tomato daily

EGGS 3 TO 5 A WEEK; 1 DAILY PREFERRED

MEAT, CHEESE, FISH, POULTRY
1 OR MORE SERVINGS DAILY
Dried beans, peas, peanuts occasionally

CEREAL AND BREAD
2 OR MORE SERVIN
Whole-grain valu
Added milk imp

BUTTER 2 OR MORE TABL

OTHER FOODS TO SATISFY
APPETITE AND COMPLETE
GROWTH AND ACTIVITY NEEDS

1992
USDA
Food Pyramid

1946
National
Nutrition Guide

REMEMBER the PYRAMID?

The USDA has been trying to help people eat a healthy diet for many years. Every so often, they change their approach. This gives them a chance to put in new information. And it lets them make the guides easier to understand.

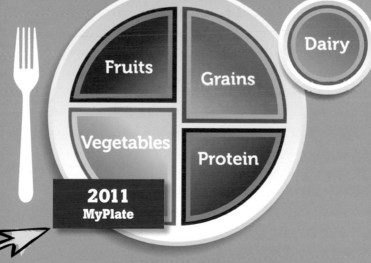

2011 MyPlate

Fruits

Grains

Dairy

Vegetables

Protein

Choose**MyPlate**.gov

Whole Grains

Not all **carbohydrates** (kahr-boh-HAHY-dreytz) are equally healthy. If a brown grain like wheat looks like a fluffy white powder, some of the nutrients may have been removed. Look for foods marked as *whole grains* to make sure you are getting all the good stuff. When in doubt, pick breads that are brown instead of white. This usually means they have more fiber and vitamins in them.

SALTY or SWEET?

Try this experiment to taste the sweet side of carbs.

| STEP 1 | Chew a soda cracker. Notice how it tastes. But don't swallow it right away. |
| STEP 2 | Keep chewing for about five minutes. |

The cracker will start to taste sweet! This is because the **saliva** in your mouth starts to change the starch in the cracker into sugar.

TASTE TEST

Our tongue is covered with taste buds. They help us tell the difference between salty, sweet, bitter, and sour foods. Our noses also play an important role in tasting food. The smell of food gives it flavor. Try this test.

STEP 1

Blindfold a friend and have him or her hold his or her nose.

STEP 2

Give your friend something to taste. Can your friend tell the difference between an apple and a pear? What about a lemon and an orange?

STEP 3

Try the same test without your friend holding his or her nose. Is it easier to guess what each food is?

HIDDEN SUGAR

Carbs aren't the only foods with a sweet side. Some foods we don't think of as sweet have a lot of sugar in them. Compare the foods below to see which have more and which have less sugar.

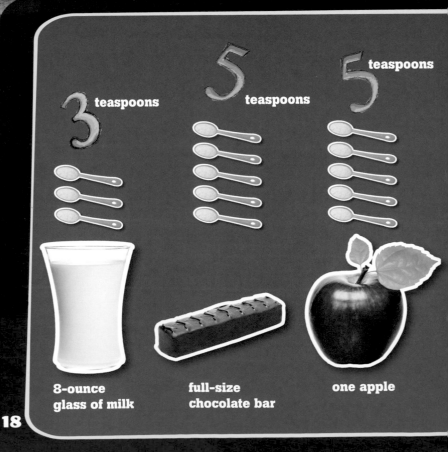

3 teaspoons

5 teaspoons

5 teaspoons

8-ounce glass of milk

full-size chocolate bar

one apple

STOP! THINK...

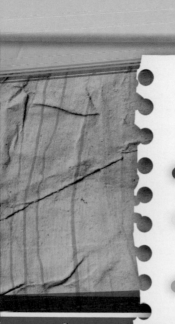

- Which foods with hidden sugars also have nutritional benefits?

- Do you think there's a difference between sugar that is added to food and sugar that is naturally in food?

- What could you do to limit the sugar from these foods?

6 teaspoons

12 teaspoons

12 teaspoons

small yogurt

bran muffin

12-ounce can of soda

Food Groups

Every food is a little different. But a grape has more in common with an apple than it does with a hunk of cheese. When deciding what to eat, it can be very helpful to put foods in groups. These groups help us know how our bodies use the foods we eat. You may have a favorite food group. But it's healthier to eat some foods from each group every day. Carbohydrates, protein, dairy, fruits, and vegetables are the main food groups.

Athletes often load up on carbohydrates before a big game or a long race because they provide energy very quickly.

High-Energy Grains

Your body uses **glucose** for energy. Most food doesn't have any glucose in it. But your body can change some foods into glucose. Proteins and fats can be changed into energy, but it takes a long time. It's easiest for your body to change carbohydrates into energy. Foods made from grains like bread, tortillas, and rice have a lot of carbs. These are high-energy foods.

A Stronger You

Everybody needs protein to stay healthy. Proteins help your body build, fix, and maintain itself. Muscles, skin, and other organs are made mostly of protein. Proteins are made of smaller **amino acids**. Your body needs 22 different amino acids to be healthy. It can make 13 of them on its own, but there are 9 you need to get from your food. Animal proteins, like meat and milk, have all nine. But many proteins that come from plants don't. People who are **vegetarians** don't eat meat. They must eat a variety of foods to get all their amino acids. Luckily, you don't need to eat all of them at the same meal. Your body will take what it needs from each meal and match the nutrients up later.

GOOD FATS and BAD FATS

Unsaturated fats and fatty acids are good for the heart. They can be found in proteins such as fish, walnuts, avocados, and many other foods. **Saturated fats** should be eaten sparingly. Too much can lead to heart disease.

COMPLETE PROTEINS

These foods or food combinations have all nine amino acids that your body needs.

➤ an egg
➤ red beans and rice
➤ a glass of low-fat milk
➤ tofu or soybeans
➤ a chicken breast or other serving of meat
➤ quinoa (KEEN-wah) (a grain that has all nine amino acids)
➤ peanut butter on a piece of whole-grain toast

**quinoa oatmeal
breakfast with raisins**

LowFat
Milk

Fruit

Fruits are a special part of a plant. They protect the seeds as they grow into new plants. Many fruits are juicy and sweet! They also usually have a lot of vitamins and minerals. And many fruits are a great source of fiber, too.

Different plants grow in different places. So, different fruits are popular in different countries. If you grew up in Southeast Asia, you might like **rambutans**. These leathery red fruits have spines on the outside. In India, **jackfruit** is common. It tastes a little like pineapple. In China, people love to eat **lychee** for dessert. They look a bit like small rambutans and are very sweet. In Mexico, people like to eat mangos and papaya.

jackfruit

rambutan

lychees

MOST POPULAR

The most popular fruit in the world is the tomato. Many people think tomatoes are vegetables, but they are really fruits. They are the part of the plant that holds the seeds. Mangos come in second. Bananas round out the top three.

WORLD'S SMELLIEST FRUIT!

The durian (DOOR-ee-uhn) fruit is popular in Asia. It has a hard, spiky skin and soft pulp in the center. It is known around the world for its intense smell. Some have compared the smell to almonds. Others say it smells more like gym socks. The smell is so strong that people are not allowed to eat it in some public places such as airports, train stations, and hotels!

durian

Vegetables

You are eating part of a plant, but it isn't a seed, grain, nut, or fruit. You are probably eating a vegetable. What do veggies bring to the table? They are high in vitamins and minerals. Some, like broccoli, have good amounts of protein, too. Vegetables also usually have a lot of fiber. The more veggies you eat, the lower your risk for many serious diseases. Some cancers and eye problems tend to happen less in people who eat a lot of vegetables.

CARROT COLORS

Carrots used to be purple! Dutch growers worked with carrots during the 1500s and 1600s until they created the juicy orange varieties we have today.

FRUIT or VEGGIE?

Which of these foods are fruits, and which are vegetables?

zucchini

tomatoes   cucumbers   peppers

pumpkins

breadfruit   eggplant

avocado   squash

tomatillos

okra

This is a trick question. They're *all* fruits! But they are used like vegetables when cooking.

KEEP IT MOVING

Fiber is found in fruits, vegetables, and whole grains. Your body can't digest it. But as it passes through you, it helps keep your digestive system healthy. If you don't eat enough fiber, you may get **constipated**. This means you may find it hard to have a bowel movement. Eating foods with fiber and drinking enough water keep your digestive system healthy.

Dairy

Dairy products include milk and things made from milk, such as cheese and yogurt. These foods are one easy way to get the **calcium** your body needs. Calcium is a mineral that makes up a large part of your bones and teeth. If you don't get enough calcium, your bones and teeth can grow weak. **Whole milk** has a lot of fat in it. It is meant to give baby cows what they need. But it has too much fat for many people. For a healthier option, choose dairy foods marked *low fat* or *nonfat*.

DID YOU KNOW?

Whole milk from cows milked in the winter has more fat in it than whole milk from cows milked in the summer.

LACTOSE

Lactose (LAK-tohs) is the main sugar in milk. Most babies digest it easily. But some people lose this ability when they are older. People who cannot digest lactose are called *lactose intolerant*. Drinking milk can make these people feel very sick. But they can still get the calcium they need by eating calcium-rich foods like broccoli, oranges, or lactose-free milk.

HOW MUCH FAT?

Food	Fat Percent by Weight
butter	80–85%
heavy cream	36–40%
whole milk	about 4%
reduced fat milk	2%
low-fat milk	1%
skim (nonfat) milk	0%

Deciding What to Eat

There are many ways to get the fuel and nutrients your body needs. A person in India probably does not eat the same foods as someone in France. But they may both have healthy diets. Most people wind up eating a combination of foods they grew up with and other foods available in their area. But how do they decide what foods to eat each day?

a traditional Ethiopian meal

Family

Your first source of information about food is your family. We tend to like the kinds of foods we grow up with. You may not like every dish. But when you are a kid, you mostly eat what your parents offer you.

Education

This book is another source of information about food. There are many books, articles, and websites with helpful information about food choices. These can help you make good choices about healthy eating.

DARE YOU!

Do you hate eating green peppers? Or fish? Or milk? It's OK to dislike some foods, but every so often, try them again. You might find that you love something you used to hate.

Health Concerns

Some people need to choose their food based on special health concerns. **Diabetes** and allergies are two common conditions.

Insulin is a chemical your body makes. Its job is to keep the amount of sugar in your blood steady. If your blood has too much sugar, your body releases insulin. The insulin helps your body store the sugar until you need it. Some people have a disease called *diabetes*. Diabetics don't make enough insulin. Diabetics must be careful about the foods they eat. They test their blood to make sure it has the right amount of sugar. Some diabetics need to inject insulin to keep their sugar levels steady.

DIABETES

Some people are born with diabetes. Other people develop it when they grow overweight. This second type of diabetes is becoming more common in children.

Portable glucose monitors allow diabetics to check insulin levels without a doctor's help.

Allergies

When someone has a food allergy, the body reacts to a normal food as though it were dangerous. Someone who is allergic may feel itchy. Allergies can also cause sore throats or stomach cramps. Some allergens can cause vomiting or difficulty breathing. Sometimes, the body reacts so strongly to the food that a doctor must treat the patient to avoid death.

USE CAUTION

Common food allergies include peanuts, eggs, beans, milk, and seafood. People with food allergies must avoid the foods they are allergic to.

Marketing

Unfortunately, many people make their food choices based on advertisements. They may not even know they are doing it. A burger looks so delicious on TV. So for the next meal, you order one. That sugary cereal has a toy in it you want. So you ask your mom if you can get a box. But, remember, the job of advertisers is to sell you things, *not* to make you healthy.

This tempting meal includes a whopping 800 calories.

ADVERTISING TRICKS

Print ads, commercials, and packaging all work on many levels to make you hungry for their product.

Everyone in the ad looks happy, healthy, and successful. Will you feel like this if you buy this food more, too?

If you buy this cereal, will you become famous like this person?

NUCLEAR

SugarBursts

Cereal looks dry and boring without milk, but milk doesn't always look good on film, and it's easy to spill. So food stylists use white glue instead!

Special lighting makes the food glow.

Community

The last big factor in the foods people choose is community. Usually, people can only get foods that are available near them. Stores go where people spend their money. So if people only eat at fast-food restaurants, that is what will be around. If they buy lots of fresh fruits and veggies, more of those will be available.

Together, we can make healthy choices. It starts on a small scale. You can help your friends be healthy. Set an example by eating healthy foods. And support your friends when they make good food choices.

Farmers markets supply a variety of fresh fruits and vegetables.

FARMERS MARKETS

Foods can lose nutrition the longer they are stored. Farmers markets are a great way to make sure you are getting foods that are fresh. These are places where farmers who are local to your community come to sell their foods. Do you have a farmers market near you?

HOW FAR DID THAT APPLE TRAVEL?

The food we buy at the store travels an average of 1,300 miles from the farm to the store! This uses a lot of **fossil fuels.** And the foods need to be carefully packaged with paper and plastics. Buying foods produced closer to home can be healthier. And it is also an environmentally friendly choice.

DIG DEEPER!

CHANGING SCHOOLS and COMMUNITIES

Jamie Oliver is a chef from England. He noticed that some towns had very high rates of **obesity.** He also noticed many schools weren't serving healthy foods at lunch. They served many high-fat foods and few fresh fruits and vegetables. So Oliver worked to change things. He taught people about nutrition. And he worked with communities to change what was offered in school lunches. People started taking control and making their communities healthier.

Oliver speaks with young chefs and students around the world.

In England, Oliver helped change the rules about what could go in school lunches. Today, he is working in America to help schools change.

GET INVOLVED

There are many other groups working to help communities eat healthy foods. Do a little research on what groups are active in your community. Talk with your parents and your school leaders about ways that you can make sure that there are healthy choices available.

The Last Bite

How can you make good choices about your diet? First, eat a variety of foods. No one food will give your body everything it needs to stay healthy and strong. Second, eat enough, but not too much. If you eat too little, your body will feel sluggish. If you eat too much, your body will store the extra as fat. Too much fat on your body isn't healthy. And finally, learn about your food options. It's easier to make good decisions when you have all the facts. To help with the last part, here is a chart with some information about common foods. Enjoy!

The RIGHT STUFF

WHAT YOU NEED	WHERE TO GET IT
Protein	seafood, meats, poultry, eggs, beans, and dairy foods
Fiber	whole grains, fruits, vegetables, beans, and nuts
Fatty Acids	flaxseed oil, nuts, avocado, spinach, and salmon
Vitamin A	papaya, watermelon, tomato, carrots, dairy, eggs, pecans, and pistachios
Vitamin B	avocado, berries, squash, corn, beans, peas, eggs, fish, milk, cheese, yogurt, and whole grains
Vitamin C	citrus fruits, papaya, chestnuts, broccoli, and brussels sprouts
Calcium	dairy products, eggs, tofu, pinto beans, broccoli, and almonds
Iron	clams, meats, cereals, edamame, pumpkin seeds, lentils, and spinach

Glossary

allergies—dangerous or irritating reactions to normal foods; symptoms may include rashes, vomiting, and difficulty breathing

amino acids—the 22 parts that make up complete proteins

calcium—a mineral found in most plants and animals that supports strong, healthy bones

calorie—the amount of energy it takes to raise the temperature of one kilogram of water by one degree Celsius, used as a measure of energy in foods

carbohydrates—high-energy foods that contain sugars and starches

constipated—unable to have a bowel movement

diabetes—a disease in which the body does not make enough insulin or does not use the insulin very well

digestive tract—the path food travels as it is broken down and absorbed by the body

fiber—a substance in food that cannot be digested but helps keep your digestive system clean and moving

fossil fuels—fuels such as coal, oil, or natural gas formed in the earth from plant or animal remains

fruit—the ripe section of sweet and pulpy seed plants

glucose—the sugar your body uses for energy

insulin—a substance made in the body that helps control glucose levels

jackfruit—a large, spiny fruit popular in India and the Philippines

lactose—a sugar found in milk

lychee—a small, sweet fruit popular in China

minerals—chemicals (such as iron or zinc) that occur naturally in certain foods and are important for good health

nutrition—the process by which an animal makes use of food substances

obesity—a condition in which people have too much fat on their bodies to be healthy

protein—a substance found in foods (such as meat, milk, eggs, and beans) that is an important part of the human diet

rambutans—large red, sweet, spiny fruits from Southeast Asia

saliva—the liquid in your mouth that starts to break down starches

saturated fats—fats that can increase the risk of heart disease

thrive—to grow and do well

unsaturated fats—fats that promote healthy hearts, found in plant foods and fish

vegetables—foods that are not nuts, beans, grains, or fruits, but that come from plants

vegetarians—people who choose not to eat meat products

vitamins—substances that are necessary in very small amounts to the nutrition of most animals and some plants

whole milk—milk without fat removed

Index

Bibliography

Goodrow, Carol. *Happy Feet, Healthy Food: Your Child's First Journal of Exercise and Healthy Eating.* **Breakaway Books, 2004.**

Use this book to record your food and exercise, and to learn new games, activities, and eating tips.

Jankowski, Connie. *Investigating the Human Body: Life Science (Science Readers).* **Teacher Created Materials Publishing, 2008.**

Discover more about how the body systems work together and why you should keep your body healthy.

Macaulay, David. *The Way We Work.* **Houghton Mifflin Books, 2008.**

Detailed descriptions accompany these elaborate color sketches of every system in the body, showing just how important it is to eat good foods.

Zinczenko, David. *Eat This, Not That! for Kids! Be the Leanest, Fittest Family on the Block!* **Rodale Incorporated, 2008.**

This book has simple food swaps that will help you make healthier choices at the supermarket and at restaurants.

More to Explore

Smash Your Food

http://foodnme.com/smash-your-food

Play the smash-your-food game to find out how much sugar, salt, and oil is hidden in your favorite foods.

Super Kids Nutrition

http://www.superkidsnutrition.com

Click on the *Super Crew for Kids* link to find out more about healthy eating and try fun activities.

USDA: Choose MyPlate

http://www.choosemyplate.gov

Check out the new portion diagram for healthy eating. It also has a Super Tracker to plan and track your diet and physical activity.

Kidnetic

http://www.kidnetic.com

Get the family involved on this cool site that covers health, nutrition, and fitness. Play games, try new recipes, and read articles to become the healthiest you that you can be!

About the Author

Stephanie Paris is a seventh generation Californian. She earned her Bachelor of Arts in psychology from the University of California, Santa Cruz, and her multiple-subject teaching credential from California State University, San Jose. She has been an elementary classroom teacher, an elementary school computer and technology teacher, a home-schooling mother, an educational activist, an educational author, a web designer, a blogger, and a Girl Scout leader. Ms. Paris loves artichokes, asparagus, oatmeal, and an occasional piece of dark chocolate!